MARINADES

Marinades

HAMLYN

First published in 1998
by Hamlyn
an imprint of Reed Consumer Books Limited
Michelin House, 81 Fulham Road, London SW3 6RB

Copyright © 1998 Reed Consumer Books Limited

ISBN 0 600 59525 0

Printed in China

Special Photography: Peter Myers
Home Economist: Sunil Vijayakar
Other Photography: James Merrell

Contents

MARINADES

A simple, aromatic marinade can transform grilled food from the simply delicious to the sublimely sensational. In essence, a marinade is a highly flavored, aromatized liquid in which food is soaked before it is cooked. Marinades have many purposes but they are usually intended to change the food being marinated in some way. Traditionally, they were used for soaking very tough, lean meat, such as venison, wild boar, and hare, before cooking. Unless the animals are young, the meats can be almost inedible unless they are marinated first in a tenderizing mixture of wine, vinegar, aromatic herbs, and spices.

Why use a marinade?

There are many reasons for marinating food, including the following:

- To allow flavors to soak into the food

- To aromatize the food

- To tenderize lean meat and game and soften the fibers

- To impregnate meat or fish with juice and oil to make it more moist

- To enhance the flavors of meat, fish, and vegetables

- To coagulate the protein in fish to be eaten raw (as in ceviche)

- To baste food and keep it moist during cooking

- To act as a short-term preservative

A tenderizing agent

The acid in a marinade, usually wine, vinegar, or citrus juice (lemon, lime, or orange juice), acts as a tenderizing agent. Marinating meat or game in wine, vinegar, or yogurt tends to check the immediate decomposition of the food and allows the acids in the marinade to start breaking down the muscle fibers into slightly less tough proteins.

A moistening agent

Adding oil or melted butter to a marinade will help to keep lean meat moist and prevent it drying out in the cooking process, especially if it's grilled over hot coals or under a broiler. Very lean meats, fish, and vegetables, require an oily marinade and frequent basting during cooking, whereas non-oily, wine- or vinegar-based marinades are more suited to meat with a high fat content.

Raw and cooked marinades

Marinades may be raw or cooked. They both contain similar ingredients, such as wine, vinegar, oil, herbs, and spices, but raw marinades are more common, especially with chicken, fish, and vegetables.

Raw marinades

The marinade ingredients are simply mixed together and then poured over the food to be marinated. Raw marinades are suitable for foods that need only a short marinating time.

Uncooked marinade for meat

For large joints of beef, lamb, or venison, which you are going to braise, you can use this uncooked marinade. Season the meat with salt and pepper and put it in a large bowl. Add a sliced carrot and onion, a bay leaf, 2 cloves, and sprigs of fresh parsley and thyme. Moisten with red or dry white wine and a few drops of brandy. Cover and leave in a cool place, turning the meat occasionally in the marinade, for about 8 hours.

Uncooked marinade for fish and chicken pieces

Season the fish or chicken with salt and pepper and transfer to a large dish. Scatter some chopped onions, minced garlic, chopped parsley (or herbs of your choice) over the top. Tuck in a bay leaf and add some good olive oil and lemon juice.

Cooked marinades

Cooked marinades impart a stronger flavor to the food being marinated and are more suited to red meat and game. The marinade ingredients are cooked and usually simmered for a period of time before being thoroughly cooled and then poured over the food to be marinated.

Cooked red wine marinade

This marinade is wonderful for flavorizing beef, lamb, and game (pheasant, venison, or quail). It adds richness and a strong, pungent flavor. Heat some olive oil in a large pan and brown a sliced carrot, a chopped onion, some diced sticks of celery and a garlic clove. Add sprigs of fresh thyme and parsley, a bay leaf, and some whole black peppercorns. Add 3 cups of red wine and ½ cup wine vinegar to the pan. Simmer for 30 minutes, then remove from the heat and let stand until completely cold. Pour the cold marinade over the meat or game and leave to marinate in a cool place for several hours.

Marinade ingredients

There are many ingredients that you can use in a marinade to impart a delicious flavor. Success depends on your flair as a cook and the way in which you marry the ingredients. As a general rule, lighter meats, such as chicken, veal, and fish, blend well with lighter ingredients-white wine, gently aromatic herbs, and fewer spices. Richer, darker meats, however, such as lamb, beef, venison, and game birds, need stronger ingredients-a robust, full-bodied red wine, pungent herbs, and aromatic spices.

Oil

All marinades for grilling must contain a good proportion of oil-to add moistness to lean meat, fish, shrimp, and vegetables, and to use during basting. The oil you use depends very much on personal preference and the type of recipe. For example, a fruity, strong, extra virgin olive oil will compliment red meat or Mediterranean vegetables (zucchini, eggplants, bell peppers, etc.), whereas a lighter peanut oil may be more suited to white fish or seafood. Chinese sesame oil, which is extracted from sesame seeds, is excellent in Oriental marinades blended with soy sauce, ginger root, chiles, and spices. Whatever oil you decide to use, it will soak into the meat and add fat to keep it soft during cooking.

Wine

Whether you use red or white wine will depend on the food being marinated. As before, white wine tends to be better with fish, seafood, and chicken, whereas red wine is more suited to stronger-tasting red meats and game. You might like to add a little fortified wine, such as port, sherry, or Madeira, for extra flavor and zing.

Vinegar

A variety of vinegars can be used, including red or white wine vinegars, apple cider vinegar, sherry vinegar, and herb vinegars. One of the oldest cooking ingredients, vinegar is a natural preservative and has been used for centuries to marinate meat, fish, and vegetables. Its acetic acid is the tenderizing agent in most marinades, making lean meat less tough.

Fruit juice

Lemon, lime, orange, and pineapple juices all add sweetness and flavor to a marinade. Because they are quite acidic, they also help tenderize the meat being marinated. In fact, the South American dish of ceviche, or escabeche, consists of raw fish which literally "cooks" in a mixture of citrus juice and vinegar — a form of chemical cooking.

Yogurt

This sour milk product is widely used in Indian and Middle Eastern marinades, usually flavored with aromatic herbs and spices, such as ground turmeric, ginger, cumin, and coriander. Yogurt contains lactic acid and marinating meat in it helps slow down the natural decomposition of the meat and also tenderizes it.

Herbs

Fresh or dried herbs add flavor and aroma to a marinade, helping to perfume the food being marinated. Almost any herb can be used. Like spices, herbs contain essential oils and many have a preservative action when used in a marinade.

- Strong, pungent herbs, such as mint and rosemary, are good with red meats, especially lamb.
- Spicy Mediterranean herbs (basil, origano, cilantro, and marjoram) compliment chicken and vegetables.
- Milder herbs, such as tarragon, dill weed, and chervil, go well with fish.
- Dried herbs have a more concentrated flavor than fresh ones and should always be used in smaller quantities.

Spices

Whole or ground, spices will lend a pungency to any marinade and should be chosen with care.

- Strong spices, such as cinnamon, cloves, ginger, allspice, and cumin, are suitable for red meats and game.
- Milder spices, such as nutmeg, coriander, and cardamom, go well with chicken, seafood, and some vegetables.

In medieval Europe, spices were valued as highly as precious metals and stones, and the spice trade flourished between the Orient and the West. Spices were used not only for their natural preserving properties but also to flavor meat, especially during the cold winter months when they were sometimes essential for disguising the taste of meat that was not fresh! Here is a brief guide to some spices that can be used in marinades:

Allspice:

These dark brown berries, which slightly resemble black peppercorns, come from an evergreen tree in the bay family. With their distinctive flavor, reminiscent of cinnamon, cloves, juniper berries, and nutmeg, they can be used whole or ground. They are very popular in the Caribbean, especially Jamaica, where they are used to season meat and chicken.

Cinnamon

The scented bark quills of the cinnamon tree, cinnamon should be bought in small quantities as it quickly loses its pungency and aroma when ground.

Cloves

In reality, these are the unopened flower buds of an evergreen tree. They are extremely strong tasting and pungent, and a little goes a long way in a marinade. Either add them whole or ground.

Coriander seeds

Sweet with a faintly orange flavor, when crushed, coriander seeds blend well with white wine and herb marinades. Mix in some bruised garlic cloves, bay leaves, and lemon juice for an excellent marinade for chicken.

Cumin

This spice is the characteristic flavoring agent in most North African and Middle Eastern dishes. The whole seeds or ground powder can be mixed into yogurt marinades for lamb and chicken.

Ginger

Fresh ginger root or powdered ginger makes a spicy addition to a marinade. It is an essential ingredient in most Oriental marinades.

Nutmeg

The aromatic nutmeg comes from the same tree as mace. Nutmeg is always at its most pungent when it is grated fresh rather than using the ground powder which tends to lose its potency with age.

Peppercorns

Whole or ground black and white peppercorns are an essential ingredient in most marinades. Black peppercorns have a more aromatic scent and flavor than white ones, which are stronger and hotter.

Soy sauce

Made from fermented soya beans, flour, and water, soy sauce is used extensively in Chinese and Japanese cooking and is often added to Oriental marinades. You can buy either light or dark soy sauce. The dark variety is mellow tasting and almost black in color, whereas the light soy is saltier and amber colored.

Salt

Fine or coarsely ground salt is a key ingredient in nearly all marinades. Salt provides a valuable function for, in addition to its characteristic flavoring, it is a natural preservative. It also helps to increase our awareness of other flavors-very important in a marinade.

Oriental flavorings

Together with soy sauce, you can add sherry, rice wine vinegar, grated fresh root ginger, hoisin sauce (a sweet sauce made from soya beans), cilantro, and hot chiles to Oriental marinades. The Thais are very partial to nam pla (a fish sauce) which they blend with lemon grass, chiles, kaffir lime leaves, and cilantro, to make a fragrant, spicy marinade for fish, shrimp, meat, and chicken.

Other flavorings

These include garlic (whole or minced), honey (to add sweetness), mustard (prepared or powdered), chopped onions, scallions, or shallots, and sliced root vegetables, such as carrots and turnips.

Marinating method

To marinate any food, place it in a ceramic or glass container, pour over the prepared marinade liquid, cover the container, and leave in a cool place or the refrigerator for the recommended time. Be sure to turn the food several times in the marinade to allow the flavors to penetrate evenly. When the marinating time is completed, remove the food from the liquid and dry it thoroughly on paper towels. This is essential with meat if it is to brown during grilling-otherwise, it will be too moist and there is a tendency to "stew" in the excess moisture.

Reserve the leftover marinade-don't throw it away. You can use it for basting the meat or fish during cooking. If the meat has been left in the refrigerator to marinate, you should allow it to come up to room temperature before cooking it, or it will be difficult to judge the cooking time accurately.

Marinating times

These vary according to the type and weight of the food being marinated and it is always best to follow the recommended times given in individual recipes. However, as a general rule of thumb, the longer a food is left in a marinade, the more flavor it absorbs. Here are some helpful guidelines:

• Fish and seafood: 2-3 hours

• Chicken and veal: 6-8 hours

• Lamb: 24 hours

• Beef and game: up to 3 days

Remember that the food being marinated will mature twice as fast if it is left to marinate at room temperature rather than in the refrigerator.

Oily and non-oily marinades

Most marinades contain some oil, in varying proportions. Oily marinades must always be used on dry or lean foods that contain little or no fat, such as lean cuts of meat, chicken, white fish, and vegetables. However, foods with a naturally high fat content, such as oily fish, may benefit from a non-oily marinade, which is based on vinegar, citrus juice, or wine.

FISH STEAKS WITH TOMATO AND GARLIC SAUCE

**4 x 5-ounce white fish steaks,
e.g. sea bass or anglerfish
3 tablespoons olive oil
1 tablespoon chopped oregano**

**Marinade:
5 tablespoons olive oil
juice of ½ lemon
1 teaspoon grated lemon zest
1 tablespoon finely chopped parsley**

**Tomato and Garlic Sauce:
2 tablespoons olive oil
4 garlic cloves, minced
1½ pounds tomatoes, skinned and chopped
4 anchovy fillets, chopped
salt and freshly ground black pepper**

1 Wash the fish steaks under running cold water and pat dry with paper towels.

2 Put all the marinade ingredients in a bowl and mix together well. Add the white fish steaks to the marinade, turning until they are thoroughly coated and glistening with oil. Cover the bowl and leave in a cool place for at least 1 hour.

3 Heat 3 tablespoons of the olive oil in a large skillet. Remove the fish steaks from the marinade and fry gently until they are cooked and golden brown on both sides, turning the fish once during cooking. Remove the steaks from the skillet and keep them warm.

4 While the fish steaks are cooking, make the Tomato Sauce. Heat the olive oil in a pan and sauté the garlic until just golden. Add the tomatoes and chopped anchovies, and cook over a moderate heat until the tomatoes are reduced to a thick pulpy consistency. Season to taste with salt and pepper. Pour the sauce over the fish and sprinkle with oregano.

Serves 4
Preparation time: 15 minutes, plus marinating
Cooking time: 15 minutes

HERB MARINADE

This marinade is particularly good with any fish that is going to be broiled or barbecued,
such as tuna or mackerel.

4 tablespoons olive oil
4 garlic cloves, minced
¹/₂ cup dry white wine
1 small onion, finely chopped
1 sprig each of fresh rosemary,
thyme, and parsley

1 Mix the olive oil, garlic, white wine, chopped onion together with the herbs.

2 Marinate the fish for several hours or overnight, or for as long as 24 hours, if possible.

Preparation time: 5 minutes, plus marinating

SOY SAUCE MARINADE WITH TUNA STEAK

This marinade would also work especially well with salmon or halibut steaks.

4 x 6-ounce tuna steaks

Soy Sauce Marinade:
2 tablespoons oil
2 tablespoons light soy sauce
1 tablespoon lemon juice
$\frac{1}{2}$ teaspoon ground cumin
1 teaspoon chopped chives,
plus extra, to serve

Avocado Sauce:
1 ripe avocado, peeled and pitted
3 tablespoons sour cream
1 teaspoon lemon juice

1 Mix all the marinade ingredients together. Put the tuna in a shallow dish, pour the marinade over the top and leave to marinate in this mixture for at least 30 minutes, or overnight.
2 Remove the steaks and reserve the marinade. If available, place the fish inside greased, hinged grills and place on the preheated oiled grill over medium hot coals. Cook for about 10–15 minutes, turning frequently and basting during cooking.
3 Meanwhile, mash the avocado in a bowl with a fork and blend in the remaining ingredients. Place a spoonful of the mixture over each steak and serve immediately with extra chives.

Serves 4

Preparation time: 5 minutes, plus marinating
Cooking time: 10–15 minutes

SWORDFISH WITH FENNEL SEEDS

Swordfish is a firm-fleshed fish that is ideal for marinating and for grilling or barbecuing.
You could serve this dish with salad and plain rice or with braised vegetables.

4 swordfish steaks, about 7–8 ounces each

Fennel Marinade:
2 teaspoons fennel seeds, crushed
finely grated zest and juice of 1 lemon
1 tablespoon capers, chopped
2 tablespoons chopped dill weed
1 teaspoon paprika
1–2 garlic cloves, minced
½ cup olive oil

1 Place the swordfish in a single layer in a shallow dish. Mix the marinade ingredients together in a jug, then pour over the fish and toss to coat well. Cover and marinate for 2–3 hours, turning the fish several times.

2 Using tongs, remove the fish from the dish, reserving the marinade. Cook the steaks on an oiled grill over hot coals for 5–7 minutes on each side, basting frequently with the marinade.

Serves 4
Preparation time: 10 minutes, plus marinating
Cooking time: 10–15 minutes

HOISIN MARINADE WITH LOBSTER

Hoisin sauce is a sweet and spicy, reddish-brown sauce made from a paste of fermented soy beans, flour, salt, sugar, garlic, and red rice.

3 pounds cooked lobster or crawfish tails
1 bundle asparagus, cut into
1½-inch lengths

Hoisin Marinade:
½ cup hoisin sauce
3 tablespoons tomato paste
2 tablespoons lemon juice
2 tablespoons honey
2 tablespoons soy sauce

1 Preheat the oven to 350°F. Remove the flesh from the lobster tails and discard the shells. Cut the tails into even medallions, about ½ inch thick.

2 Place the medallions in a shallow ovenproof dish. Combine the marinade ingredients and pour them over the lobster. Cover and refrigerate for 1 hour.

3 Cook the cut asparagus in boiling lightly salted water for about 5 minutes, until it is just tender. Drain and add to the lobster. Place the dish in the preheated oven and cook for 10 minutes, or until heated through. Serve immediately.

Serves 4
Preparation time: 20 minutes, plus marinating
Cooking time: 15 minutes
Oven temperature: 350°F

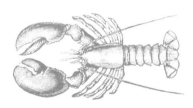

SHRIMP KEBOBS

Cubed white fish or scallops can be used instead of shrimp. Cherry tomatoes, pieces of onion or
bell pepper, and mushrooms all make attractive additions to the kebobs.

**12 jumbo shrimp, cleaned
(thawed if frozen)**
³/₄ cup long-grain rice
1¹/₂ cups frozen peas
**8 bacon slices, halved lengthwise
and rolled up**
¹/₂ stick butter
1 cup sliced mushrooms
salt and freshly ground black pepper

Balsamic Marinade:
5 tablespoons olive oil
2 tablespoons balsamic vinegar
**2 tablespoons chopped oregano
or marjoram**
2 garlic cloves, minced
freshly ground black pepper

1 To make the marinade, combine in a bowl the oil, vinegar, oregano or marjoram, garlic, and season with a little pepper.
2 Add the shrimp to the marinade, turning to coat thoroughly. Cover and leave to marinate for 1 hour.
3 Put the rice in a large saucepan of boiling salted water and cook for 12–15 minutes, or until it is just tender. Then pour into a colander to drain.
4 Cook the peas in a separate saucepan of simmering salted water for about 5 minutes, or until they are just tender, then drain thoroughly and set aside.
5 Remove the shrimp, reserving the marinade, and thread them onto 4 long kebob skewers, alternating with the rolls of bacon. Cook on an oiled barbecue for 8–10 minutes, turning the skewers several times and brushing the shrimp and bacon with the remaining marinade, until the shrimp are tender and cooked through and the bacon is crisp. Alternatively, cook under a preheated hot broiler for the same time.
6 Meanwhile, melt the butter in a saucepan, add the mushrooms, and fry gently for about 3 minutes, until colored. Stir the rice and peas into the pan and season to taste with salt and pepper.
7 Pile the rice mixture on to a heated serving dish and arrange the kebobs alongside. Serve immediately.

Serves 4
Preparation time: 15 minutes, plus marinating
Cooking time: 30 minutes

LIME MARINADE WITH SEARED PEPPER TUNA

Tuna, lightly seared outside, rare inside, is served with homemade pickled ginger. Wasabi, a hot Japanese horseradish paste available from some gourmet food stores, may also be served.

Lime Marinade:
2 tablespoons freshly squeezed lime juice
5 tablespoons peanut oil
2 garlic cloves, minced

Pickled Ginger:
6 tablespoons rice vinegar
1 tablespoon sugar
1 teaspoon salt
1 x 1-inch piece fresh ginger root, peeled and cut into wafer-thin slices

4 tuna steaks, skinned, about 6 ounces each
8 ounces rice noodles
1½ tablespoons sesame oil
2½ tablespoons sesame seeds, toasted
4 tablespoons dried pink peppercorns, crushed
salt

1 First make the marinade. Combine the lime juice, peanut oil, garlic, and salt to taste in a shallow dish, large enough to hold all the tuna in a single layer. Add the tuna, toss lightly until coated, cover the dish and marinate for 1 hour, turning once.

2 To prepare the Pickled Ginger, place the rice vinegar, sugar, and salt in a small saucepan. Bring to the boil, add the sliced ginger, lower the heat and simmer for about 1–2 minutes. Remove from the heat, transfer to a bowl and leave to cool.

3 Prepare the noodles according to the packet instructions. Drain and refresh under cold water, then drain well again. Tip the noodles into a bowl, add the sesame oil and 1½ tablespoons of the sesame seeds and toss lightly.

4 Place the peppercorns on a plate. Drain the tuna, discarding the marinade. Roll the edges of each tuna steak in the peppercorns to coat them. Sprinkle with a little salt.

5 Cook the tuna steaks on an oiled grill over moderately hot coals for 1 minute on each side to sear the edges. Slice thinly and serve with the pickled ginger and noodles, and sprinkled with the reserved sesame seeds.

Serves 4
Preparation time: 20 minutes, plus marinating
Cooking time: 2 minutes

TUNA WITH TERIYAKI MARINADE

I pound tuna fillet

Teriyaki Marinade:
I x ³/₄-inch piece fresh ginger root,
finely grated
2 tablespoons soy sauce
I tablespoon lemon juice
2 tablespoons dry sherry
¹/₂ cup fish broth

1 Remove any skin from the tuna fillet and cut into 4 even pieces.
2 In a shallow dish, combine all the marinade ingredients. Place the fillets in the marinade and set aside for at least 30 minutes, turning the tuna occasionally.
3 Place the tuna on a broiler pan, lined with kitchen foil, and cook until the flesh flakes, approximately 2–3 minutes on each side. Baste the tuna during cooking, using all the marinade. Alternatively, grill over hot coals. Serve immediately.

Serves 4
Preparation time: 10 minutes, plus marinating
Cooking time: 10 minutes

GRILLED SCALLOPS WITH COCONUT BUTTER MARINADE

The scallops need only a short time to just cook them through,
since they become tough and chewy if over-cooked.

**12 large sea scallops, washed and dried,
grey membranes removed
12 cherry tomatoes, halved
salt and freshly ground black pepper**

**Coconut Butter Marinade:
2 garlic cloves, minced
1 x ½-inch piece fresh ginger root, peeled
and very finely shredded
2 tablespoons freshly squeezed lime juice
2 teaspoons grated lemon zest
1–2 red chilies, seeded and finely chopped
½ cup coconut cream**

**To Garnish:
1 tablespoon chopped parsley
1 small red chili, finely diced
lemon wedges (optional)**

1 Mix together the marinade ingredients and place in a dish with the scallops. Cover and leave to marinate for 1–2 hours.

2 Preheat a skillet or grilling pan. Remove the scallops from the marinade and add to the pan with the tomatoes. Grill for about 3–6 minutes on each side.

3 Serve immediately, garnished with the chopped parsley, diced chili and lemon wedges, if using.

Serves 2–4

Preparation time: 10 minutes, plus marinating
Cooking time: 3–6 minutes

GINGER AND SAKE MARINADE WITH MACKEREL

Tatsuta-age is a Japanese method of frying. In this recipe the fish is marinated before frying to give it extra flavor. To obtain ginger juice, grate some fresh ginger root, then squeeze out the juice.

2 medium mackerel, total weight about 1½ pounds, filleted
4 tablespoons shoyu (Japanese soy sauce)
2 tablespoons sake (rice wine)
1 teaspoon fresh ginger juice
cornstarch, for coating
8 small button mushrooms, trimmed
oil for deep-frying

Garnish:
4 lemon wedges
1 x 2-inch piece daikon (Japanese radish), peeled and grated

1 Using tweezers, remove all the bones from the center of the mackerel fillets. Place the fillets, skin side down, on a board and cut slightly on the diagonal into the slices, about 1 inch thick.

2 Put the shoyu in a shallow dish with the sake and ginger juice and mix well. Add the mackerel slices, cover, and leave to marinate for about 10 minutes, stirring occasionally to insure the slices of fish are evenly coated. Drain the mackerel thoroughly and coat the slices in some of the cornstarch.

3 Heat the oil in a deep-fat fryer or deep skillet to 325°F, or until a cube of bread browns in 45 seconds. Deep-fry the mackerel slices until they are golden brown. Remove from the oil and drain on paper towels. Keep hot in a warm oven.

4 Coat the mushrooms in a little cornstarch. Add to the hot oil and deep-fry for 1 minute. Remove and drain on paper towels.

5 Arrange a few slices of mackerel and 2 mushrooms on each of the warmed individual plates. Garnish each serving with a lemon wedge, and some of the grated daikon. Serve immediately.

Serves 4
Preparation time: 15 minutes, plus marinating
Cooking time: 6 minutes

MARINATED SALMON STEAKS WITH CAPERS

6 x 6-ounce salmon steaks

Marinade:
6 tablespoons capers
4 tablespoons olive oil
juice of 1 lemon
1 small onion, grated
3 shallots, finely chopped
1 teaspoon fresh thyme
2 bay leaves
salt and freshly ground black pepper

1 Mix the ingredients for the marinade together, beating to combine them. Place in a shallow dish with the salmon steaks and leave to marinate for 2 hours.

2 Drain the salmon steaks and grill over medium hot coals for 15–20 minutes, basting with the marinade and turning from time to time. Serve hot with any remaining marinade.

Serves 6
Preparation time: 5 minutes, plus marinating
Cooking time: 20 minutes

JUNIPER AND PEPPERCORN MARINADE
WITH BUTTERFLIED SALMON

1 x 4–5-pound salmon, scaled, cleaned, and head removed

Juniper and Peppercorn Marinade:
1½ tablespoons dried juniper berries
2 teaspoons dried green peppercorns
¼ teaspoon black peppercorns
1 teaspoon sugar
2–3 tablespoons vegetable oil

To Garnish:
1–2 green onions, shredded
lemon slices
frilly lettuce leaves

1 When you buy the salmon, ask the person serving you to butterfly and bone it for you.

2 Coarsely grind the juniper berries and green and black peppercorns in a spice grinder, or use a mortar and pestle. Mix with the sugar and oil.

3 Open the salmon like a book, flesh side up, and pull out any remaining bones with tweezers. Brush over the juniper-oil mixture. Close up the salmon again and place it in a dish. Cover closely and marinate in the refrigerator for 2 hours.

4 About 15 minutes before cooking, remove the salmon from the refrigerator and open it up again. Place it, flesh side up, on a baking dish. Brush over any left-over marinade. Cook under a preheated broiler, about 5–6 inches from the source of heat, for 8–10 minutes, or until the salmon flakes easily when tested with a fork or skewer. Do not overcook it or the fish will become dry. Garnish with the shredded green onions, slices of lemon and lettuce leaves. Serve hot.

Serves 6–8
Preparation time: 10 minutes, plus marinating
Cooking time: 8–10 minutes

GRAPEFRUIT MARINATED PORK KEBOBS

These spicy kebobs are delicious with cold ratatouille and baked potatoes, or hot French bread and a green salad.

3 pounds boned lean pork, cut into cubes
salt and freshly ground black pepper
plain yogurt, to serve

Grapefruit Marinade:
6 tablespoons vegetable oil
finely grated zest and juice
of 1½ grapefruits
3 tablespoons dark brown sugar
3 tablespoons soy sauce
2 tablespoons molasses
3 fresh green chilis, finely chopped
1 x 2-inch piece fresh ginger root, peeled,
chopped, and pounded to a paste
1 teaspoon hot pepper sauce

1 Place the pork in a large bowl and season with salt and pepper. Combine all the ingredients for the marinade, stirring until thoroughly mixed. Pour the marinade over the pork and stir well so that each piece of meat is thoroughly coated with the marinade. Refrigerate for 24 hours, stirring the meat from time to time. Let stand at room temperature for 1–2 hours before cooking.

2 Thread the pork cubes on to 8–10 oiled metal skewers. Place the kebobs on a grill over medium hot coals and cook for approximately 20 minutes, turning the kebobs frequently and brushing the pork with the remaining marinade. Alternatively, cook under a preheated hot broiler for the same time. Serve immediately with a bowl of plain yogurt.

Serves 4–6

Preparation time: 10 minutes, plus marinating and standing
Cooking time: 20 minutes

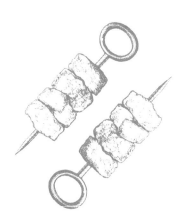

PINEAPPLE AND MOLASSES MARINADE WITH BEEF KEBOBS

I pound lean steak or beef fillet,
fat removed
3 tomatoes
2 onions
I green bell pepper
12 pineapple cubes, fresh or canned
boiled rice, to serve

Pineapple and Molasses Marinade:
I tablespoon molasses
4 tablespoons pineapple juice
2 tablespoons wine vinegar
I tablespoon oil
salt and freshly ground black pepper

1 Make the marinade: put the molasses, pineapple juice, wine vinegar, and oil in a bowl and mix well together. Add a little salt and some black pepper.

2 Cut the steak into 1-inch cubes and add to the marinade. Cover and leave in a cool place for at least 1 hour. Remove the steak and reserve the marinade for basting the kebobs.

3 Cut the tomatoes into quarters. Peel the onions and cut them into small chunks. Remove the core and seeds from the green bell pepper, and cut it into squares.

4 Thread the steak, tomatoes, onions, bell pepper, and pineapple chunks alternately on to 4 long or 8 short skewers. Brush them with the reserved marinade. Cook under a hot broiler or over hot coals for about 10 minutes, turning frequently and basting often. Serve with plain boiled rice with the remaining marinade poured over the top.

Serves 4
Preparation time: 15 minutes, plus marinating
Cooking time: 10 minutes

MEXICAN MARINADE AND HAMBURGERS

I pound ground beef
I egg, beaten
I tablespoon oil
½ teaspoon chili powder

Mexican Marinade:
4 green onions, washed and chopped
4 tablespoons white wine
2 tablespoons wine vinegar
I teaspoon chopped tarragon
salt and freshly ground black pepper

To Serve:
hamburger buns
a few lettuce leaves
I small tomato, sliced
I small onion, cut into rings
I avocado, peeled, halved, and pitted, half diced and half sliced
pickles, sliced
ketchup (optional)
paprika, for sprinkling

I Make the marinade: mix the green onions, wine, vinegar, tarragon and salt and pepper, to taste. Marinate the ground beef in this mixture for several hours. Remove the beef and drain thoroughly, discarding the marinade.

2 Place the beef in a bowl and add the beaten egg. Form the beef into 4 burgers. Heat the oil in a large skillet, sprinkle with chili powder, and brown for about 5 minutes on each side.

3 Serve on a hamburger bun, toasted if liked, with the lettuce, sliced tomato, onion rings and sliced and diced avocado, sprinkled with paprika. You could even accompany the burgers with some sliced pickles and ketchup, if liked.

Serves 4
Preparation time: 15 minutes, plus marinating
Cooking time: about 10 minutes

SOUR CREAM MARINADE WITH KEBOBS

In addition, use this marinade for steak, lamb chops, turkey or chicken, allowing 2–4 hours to marinate, depending on the size of the meat.

2 lb boned leg of veal, cut into 1-inch cubes
1 large eggplant, cubed
12 small onions
12 bay leaves
lemon juice
salt and freshly ground black pepper

Sour Cream Marinade:
$1/2$ cup sour cream
1 tablespoon lemon juice
1 garlic clove, minced
1 celery stalk, thinly sliced
large pinch of paprika
$1/2$ teaspoon Worcestershire sauce

1 First make the marinade. Put the sour cream into a bowl and add the lemon juice, garlic, celery, paprika, and Worcestershire sauce. Mix well to combine.

2 Place the veal cubes in a shallow dish and pour the marinade over, covering well. Leave to marinate in the refrigerator for 3–4 hours, turning occasionally.

3 Meanwhile, put the eggplant cubes in a colander and sprinkle with a little salt. Leave to stand for about 30 minutes, then rinse and pat dry with paper towels. Sprinkle the eggplant with a little lemon juice and salt and pepper.

4 Blanch the onions in boiling water for 1–3 minutes and then drain well.

5 Remove the veal from the marinade and thread onto oiled skewers, alternating with the eggplant, onions and bay leaves. Cook under a hot broiler or over hot coals for about 15 minutes, turning frequently.

Serves 2–4
Preparation time: 5 minutes
Cooking time: about 15 minutes

SAUCY BARBECUED PORK

6 x 6-ounce pork chops

Barbecue Marinade:
I teaspoon mustard powder
I teaspoon salt
½ teaspoon chili powder
I tablespoon firmly packed dark brown sugar
I x 10-ounce can condensed tomato soup
2 tablespoons vinegar
2 tablespoons Worcestershire sauce
2 tablespoons soy sauce

I Place the pork chops in a shallow dish. In a separate bowl, mix all the marinade ingredients together and pour over to cover the meat. Leave in a cool place to marinate for at least 1–2 hours.
2 Remove the meat and reserve the marinade. Place the chops on a well-oiled grill over hot coals and cook for about 5 minutes each side, basting with the remaining marinade. Alternatively, cook under a preheated hot grill. Serve hot.

Serves 6
Preparation time: 5 minutes, plus marinating
Cooking time: 10 minutes

COLD BEEF WITH REDCURRANTS

Perfect for a cold lunch or picnic, this salted beef is fully cooked, sliced, and covered with a fruit sauce to keep it moist and tasty.

I x 3¹/₂-pound piece rolled salted beef
2 cups water
¹/₂ pound baby carrots, scraped
¹/₂ pound redcurrants
4 tablespoons cranberry jelly
I tablespoon Worcestershire sauce
few sprigs of fresh herbs, to serve

White Wine Marinade:
¹/₂ cup sweet vermouth
I¹/₄ cups sweet white wine
chopped parsley, to garnish

1 Put the meat into a dish with the marinade ingredients and leave to marinate for 1–2 hours. Transfer the meat to a saucepan, pour over the marinade and add the water, baby carrots, and half of the redcurrants.

2 Bring to the boil, then lower the heat, cover the pan, and simmer for 3 hours, or until the beef is very tender. Cool quickly in the cooking liquid.

3 Remove the beef from the cooking liquid and slice thinly, discarding the kitchen string but reserving the cooking liquid. Overlap the slices on a serving platter and add the carrots.

4 Meanwhile, put the cranberry jelly and Worcestershire sauce in a small pan and heat gently, stirring until the jelly has melted. Strain the reserved cooking liquid from the beef and stir 1¹/₄ cups of liquid into the sauce in the pan. Add the remaining cranberries (reserving 1 sprig for serving), bring to a boil, then simmer for 3 minutes, until the berries start to burst. Remove from the heat, cover the pan, and set aside until the sauce is cold.

5 Serve the cold sliced beef with the cold sauce and reserved cranberries and garnish with parsley.

Serves 6
Preparation time: 15 minutes, plus marinating and standing
Cooking time: 3 hours

VENISON WITH RED WINE AND COGNAC MARINADE

2½ pounds stewing venison,
cut into 1-inch cubes

2 tablespoons all-purpose flour

3 tablespoons olive oil

6 ounces bacon slices, cut into strips

2 onions, chopped

2 garlic cloves, minced

2 cups game or beef broth or water

1 sprig of rosemary

1 sprig of thyme

1 bay leaf

6 juniper berries, crushed

salt and freshly ground black pepper

Red Wine and Cognac Marinade:

1¼ cups red wine

1 onion, chopped

3 tablespoons Cognac

2 tablespoons olive oil

Cranberry Balls:

1½ cups fresh or frozen cranberries,
defrosted if frozen

2 tablespoons sugar

1 cup self-rising flour, sifted

1 cup fresh white bread crumbs

3 tablespoons chopped suet

2 tablespoons chopped parsley

1 Place the venison in a large bowl, add all the marinade ingredients, stir well, cover and leave in the refrigerator to marinate for 12–24 hours.

2 Remove the venison from the marinade and pat dry with paper towels. Season the flour with salt and pepper and roll the meat in the flour, shaking off any excess. Strain the marinade, discarding the onion and reserving the liquid.

3 Heat the oil in a flameproof casserole over a moderate heat, add the venison, in batches, and brown well all over. Remove the browned meat with a slotted spoon and set aside.

4 Add the bacon to the casserole and cook for 3–4 minutes, until lightly browned. Add the onions and garlic and cook stirring, for 8–10 minutes, until softened.

5 Pour in the reserved marinade liquid, bring to a boil, and boil rapidly until reduced by one-third. Return the venison to the casserole with any meat juices. Stir in the broth or water, rosemary, thyme, bay leaf, and juniper berries. Bring to the boil, cover tightly and simmer gently for 1½–2 hours, until the meat is tender. Alternatively, cook in a preheated oven at 325°F.

6 To make the cranberry balls, put the cranberries and sugar in a small pan with 1 tablespoon water. Bring to a boil and simmer gently for 1–2 minutes, until the berries start to burst.

7 Mix together the flour, bread crumbs, suet, and parsley. Season to taste and stir in the cranberries, adding more water if needed, to make a soft dough. Form into 8 small balls and add to the casserole for the last 15–20 minutes. Cover and cook until risen and fluffy.

Serves 4

Preparation time: 35 minutes, plus marinating
Cooking time: 1¾–2¼ hours
Oven temperature: 325°F

HONEY SAUCE

This sauce can also be used immediately as a basting sauce for chicken, duck, pork ribs, or lamb.

2 tablespoons oil
I onion, finely chopped
I garlic clove, minced
4 tablespoons orange juice
2 tablespoons clear honey
3 tablespoons wine vinegar
I tablespoon Worcestershire sauce
I teaspoon horseradish sauce
I teaspoon dry mustard
large pinch of dried rosemary
large pinch of dried thyme
salt and freshly ground black pepper

I Heat the oil in a saucepan and add the onion and garlic. Cook gently over a low heat until soft but not brown.

2 Stir in the remaining ingredients with salt and pepper to taste and simmer for 5 minutes.

3 Allow to cool for 4–6 hours in the refrigerator before using as a marinade.

Makes I¼ cups
Preparation time: 5 minutes, plus marinating
Cooking time: 10 minutes

SHISH KEBOBS

This delicious spiced marinade is easy to perfect at home. Serve as part of a meal, or with a salad, as an appetizer.

Marinade:
I onion, chopped
2 teaspoons lemon juice
2 teaspoons medium or hot curry powder
I tablespoon plain yogurt
I tablespoon garam masala
I garlic clove, finely chopped
I egg, beaten
2 tablespoons all-purpose flour
2 tablespoons chopped cilantro
¹/₂ teaspoon salt

I lb minced lamb
oil for brushing
chopped cilantro, to garnish
strips of I small red bell pepper and
I small red onion, to serve
lime quarters (optional)

1 In a large bowl, mix together all the marinade ingredients until smooth and well combined.

2 Divide the lamb into 6 portions and form into sausage shapes. Thread onto 6 oiled skewers and add to the marinade mixture. Refrigerate for at least 2–4 hours.

3 Remove the lamb kebobs from the marinade. Discard the marinade and brush the lamb with oil and cook on an oiled grill over medium hot coals for 15–20 minutes, turning occasionally. Alternatively, cook under a preheated hot broiler.

4 Garnish with the chopped cilantro and a sprinkle of curry powder for added color. Serve with the strips of bell pepper and onion and lime quarters, if liked.

Serves 2–4
Preparation time: 10 minutes, plus marinating
Cooking time: 15–20 minutes

TANDOORI CHICKEN

Instructions are given here for cooking the chicken on the grill until it is deliciously charred, but it can be cooked under the broiler. Small clay tandoori ovens are available at specialist stores, but they do not achieve the same results as the ones in Indian restaurants, which cook at searingly high temperatures.

Tandoori Marinade:
1 hot red chili, seeded and chopped
2 garlic cloves, coarsely chopped
1 x 1-inch piece fresh ginger root, coarsely chopped
2 tablespoons lemon juice
1 tablespoon coriander seeds
1 tablespoon cumin seeds
2 teaspoons garam masala
6 tablespoons plain yogurt
a few drops each of red and yellow food coloring

4 chicken portions, skinned
salt

To Garnish:
lemon wedges
sprigs of cilantro

1 Put the chili, garlic, ginger, and lemon juice in an electric spice grinder with the coriander and cumin seeds and garam masala, and process to a paste. Alternatively, pound in a pestle and mortar. Transfer the spice paste to a shallow dish in which the chicken portions will fit in a single layer. Add the yogurt, food colorings, and $\frac{1}{2}$ teaspoon salt, and stir well to mix. Set aside.

2 Slash the flesh of the chicken deeply with a sharp pointed knife, cutting down as far as the bone. Put the chicken in a single layer in the dish, then spoon the marinade over the top, brushing it into the cuts in the chicken. Cover and marinate in the refrigerator for at least 4 hours, but preferably overnight.

3 Put the chicken on a grill over hot coals. Cook, turning frequently, for 30 minutes, or until the juices run clear when the chicken is pierced with a skewer or fork. Alternatively, cook under a preheated hot broiler. Serve hot, garnished with lemon wedges and cilantro sprigs.

4 This dish tastes great accompanied by a salad of shredded lettuce, white cabbage, and raw onion slices.

Serves 4
Preparation time: 20 minutes, plus marinating
Cooking time: 40 minutes

JAMAICAN JERK CHICKEN

Jerk pork is one of Jamaica's most famous national dishes. It is cooked over hot coals at roadside shacks all over the island. Here, chicken drumsticks are "jerked" instead of pork, making perfect outdoor food to eat with your fingers. In winter, the chicken can be cooked under the broiler.

12 chicken drumsticks

Jerk Marinade:
2 tablespoons oil
I small onion, chopped finely
10 allspice berries
2 red hot chilies, seeded and coarsely chopped
juice of I lime
I teaspoon salt

1 Put all the marinade ingredients, except the chicken drumsticks, in a food processor or spice grinder and grind to a paste. Alternatively, pound in a pestle and mortar.

2 Slash the chicken drumsticks deeply with a sharp pointed knife, cutting right down as far as the bone. Coat the chicken with the jerk seasoning mixture, brushing it into the cuts in the meat so that the flavor will penetrate. Cover and leave to marinate in the refrigerator overnight.

3 Put the drumsticks on a grill over hot coals. Cook, turning frequently, for about 20 minutes, until the chicken is charred on the outside and no longer pink on the inside. Serve hot, warm, or cold.

Serves 4–6
Preparation time: 15 minutes, plus marinating
Cooking time: 20 minutes

SPICY CHICKEN SATAY

8 chicken wing joints
I teaspoon soft brown sugar
salt and freshly ground black pepper

Spicy Marinade:
I tablespoon ground almonds
I tablespoon ground ginger
I teaspoon ground coriander
pinch of chili powder
I teaspoon turmeric
I¼ cups coconut milk
I small red bell pepper, seeded,
and finely chopped

Satay Sauce:
2 onions, coarsely chopped
¾ cup roasted peanuts
pinch of chili powder
2 tablespoons oil
½ cup water
I teaspoon sugar
I tablespoon soy sauce
juice of ½ lemon

To Serve:
lettuce leaves
lemon wedges
I red and I yellow bell pepper, finely diced

1 Sprinkle the chicken with salt and pepper and place in a shallow dish. In a bowl, mix together the ground almonds, ginger, coriander, chili, and turmeric, then gradually add the coconut milk. Pour the mixture over the chicken and leave to marinate for about 2 hours.

2 Meanwhile, make the Satay Sauce. Place half of the chopped onions in a blender or food processor, add the peanuts and chili powder and process until the mixture is reduced to a paste. Heat the oil in a saucepan, add the remaining onions and sauté until soft. Add the peanut paste and cook, stirring, for 3 minutes. Gradually add the water, stirring all the time. Stir in the sugar and cook for 5 minutes. Add the soy sauce and lemon juice and stir. Keep hot.

3 Drain the chicken and reserve the marinade. Sprinkle with the brown sugar and cook on an oiled grill over medium hot coals for about 15–20 minutes, until the chicken is cooked and crisp. Alternatively, cook under a preheated hot broiler. Turn frequently and baste with the marinade. Serve on a bed of lettuce, with the lemon wedges, diced peppers and satay sauce.

Serves 4
Preparation time: 15 minutes, plus marinating
Cooking time: 15–20 minutes

YAKITORI CHICKEN

Yakitori is the Japanese version of kebobs. Cook the skewered chicken under the broiler, or on a grill over hot coals for an authentic charred look.

1 pound chicken breast fillets, skinned and boned
green onions, to garnish

Marinade:
1 x 2-inch piece fresh ginger root
4 garlic cloves, peeled
8 black peppercorns
½ cup shoyu (Japanese soy sauce)
½ cup sake (Japanese rice wine)
2 tablespoons soft brown sugar
1 tablespoon oil

1 Crush the ginger root to a paste with the garlic cloves and black peppercorns.

2 Put the shoyu, sake, soft brown sugar, and oil in a shallow dish. Add the ginger and garlic paste and beat to combine.

3 Cut the chicken breast fillets diagonally into thin strips. Add to the marinade, cover, and marinate at room temperature for at least 30 minutes. Meanwhile, soak 16 bamboo skewers in some warm water. This will prevent them from burning during cooking.

4 Drain the skewers, then thread the chicken strips onto them, and cook on an oiled grill over hot coals for 8–10 minutes, until the chicken is tender. Turn the skewers and baste the chicken with the marinade frequently during cooking. Serve hot, garnished with green onions.

Serves 4
Preparation time: 15 minutes, plus marinating
Cooking time: 8–10 minutes

ORANGE GLAZE MARINADE WITH CHICKEN

4 chicken halves, skinned
salt and freshly ground black pepper

Orange Marinade:
4 tablespoons honey
juice of ½ lemon
grated zest of 1 orange
juice of 2 oranges
2 tablespoons Worcestershire sauce
1 tablespoon soy sauce

1 Combine all the marinade ingredients in a saucepan and heat gently for 2 minutes. Allow to cool. Place the chicken in a shallow dish. Pour the marinade over the chicken and leave in a cool place to marinate for 12–24 hours, turning occasionally.

2 Remove the chicken and reserve the marinade. Place the chicken in a roasting pan and cook in a preheated oven at 350°F for about 1 hour.

3 Remove the chicken from the oven and brush with the reserved marinade. Sprinkle with salt and pepper to taste. Place on an oiled grill over medium hot coals. Cook for about 10–15 minutes, brushing with the marinade and turning frequently until the chicken is well glazed and crisp. Serve hot, accompanied with baked potatoes, if liked.

Serves 4–6
Preparation time: 10 minutes, plus marinating
Cooking time: 1¼ hours
Oven temperature: 350°F

SPICY DUCK IN PORT AND GINGER MARINADE

4 lb duck, cut into 8 pieces
1 onion, chopped
1–2 garlic cloves, minced
17 fl oz chicken or veal stock
12 ripe figs
salt and freshly ground black pepper

Port and Ginger Marinade:
14 fl oz port
4 whole star anise
2-inch piece of cinnamon stick
4 cloves
8 Szechuan or black peppercorns
2 tablespoons chopped stem ginger
4 tablespoons honey
1 piece of dried or fresh orange
or tangerine peel
1 bay leaf
1 sprig of thyme

1 Place the duck in a large bowl, add the combined marinade ingredients, stir well, cover and leave in the refrigerator to marinate for at least 2 hours or overnight.

2 Remove the duck from the marinade and pat dry. Heat a large flameproof casserole dish over a moderate heat, add the duck, a few pieces at a time, skin side down first, and brown well all over. Transfer each batch to a colander to drain. Pour off most of the fat that has rendered from the duck, leaving about 1 tablespoon in the casserole dish.

3 Add the onion and garlic to the casserole dish and cook gently for 5 minutes until softened. Return the duck pieces to the dish, pour in the marinade, bring to a boil and add the stock. Bring back to a boil, reduce the heat and season. Cover with a tight-fitting lid and simmer gently for 45 minutes.

4 Remove the lid, skim off any fat and lay the figs on top. Cover and cook for a further 20–30 minutes until the meat and figs are just tender.

5 Remove the meat and figs from the casserole and keep warm. Remove the star anise, cinnamon, bay leaf, and thyme. Skim off as much fat as possible. Increase the heat and boil rapidly until the sauce is reduced by half. Serve the duck with the warm ginger marinade and cooked figs and the stem ginger.

Serves 4
Preparation time: 30 minutes, plus marinating
Cooking time: 1½ hours

VARIATION
You could substitute 4 small ripe pears, peeled, cored and quartered, for the ripe figs.

CHARGRILLED DUCK WITH PINEAPPLE SALSA MARINADE

2 boneless duck breasts
1 x 8-ounce can pineapple slices in natural juice
2 tablespoons virgin olive oil
mixed lettuce leaves, to serve

Pineapple Salsa Marinade:
2 red chilies, seeded and finely chopped
1 garlic clove, crushed
1 tablespoon extra virgin olive oil
½ teaspoon sugar
salt and freshly ground black pepper

1 Put the duck breasts skin-side down on a board, cover with greaseproof paper and pound with a rolling pin to flatten them slightly. Remove the paper and turn the breasts skin-side up. Score the skin diagonally or in a criss-cross pattern with a very sharp knife. Place the duck skin-side up in a shallow dish.

2 Drain the pineapple slices and mix the juice with the olive oil and salt and pepper to taste. Pour over the duck, then cover and marinate for about 1 hour.

3 Meanwhile, make the pineapple salsa. Finely chop the pineapple pieces and place them in a bowl with the chilies, garlic, olive oil, sugar, and salt and pepper to taste. Stir well to mix, then cover and chill in the refrigerator until ready to serve.

4 Brush a ridged cast iron pan very lightly with olive oil and place over a moderate heat until hot. Remove the duck breasts from the marinade and place them skin-side down on the pan. Cook for about 5 minutes, pressing very firmly with a metal spatula to keep the breasts as flat as possible.

5 Drain off the excess fat and turn the duck breasts over. Cook for a further 7–8 minutes or until the duck is done to your liking (duck breasts are best served rare). Transfer the duck to a board and slice very thinly on the diagonal, removing and discarding the skin if preferred. Serve on a bed of salad leaves, with the salsa alongside.

Serves 2
Preparation time: 15 minutes, plus marinating
Cooking time: 12–13 minutes

SWEET AND SOUR CHICKEN DRUMSTICKS

8 chicken drumsticks

Sweet and Sour Marinade:
4 tablespoons tomato ketchup
2 tablespoons Worcestershire sauce
2 tablespoons white wine vinegar
2 tablespoons honey
2 tablespoons soft brown sugar

1 Slash the chicken drumsticks deeply with a sharp knife, cutting through to the bone.

2 Make the marinade by mixing together the tomato ketchup, Worcestershire sauce, wine vinegar, honey, and soft brown sugar. Put the drumsticks in a shallow dish and brush the sweet and sour mixture all over them. Cover and marinate in the refrigerator for at least 4 hours, preferably overnight.

3 Put the drumsticks on an oiled grill over hot charcoal or under a preheated broiler and cook, turning frequently, for about 20 minutes, until the chicken is charred on the outside and no longer pink on the inside. Serve the drumsticks hot or cold.

Serves 4
Preparation time: 15 minutes, plus marinating
Cooking time: 20 minutes

SESAME MARINADE WITH TURKEY

1 pound boned, skinned turkey breast,
cut into cubes
1 tablespoon oil
¾ cup unsalted cashews
3 ounces button or shiitake
mushrooms, halved

Sesame Marinade:
3 green onions, chopped
3 tablespoons soy sauce
2 tablespoons hot pepper oil
2 tablespoons sesame seed oil
1 tablespoon sesame seed paste
1 teaspoon ground Szechuan peppercorns

To Serve:
1–2 finely shredded green onions
1 finely shredded red bell pepper

1 Put the marinade ingredients in a bowl. Add the turkey cubes, turning them in the marinade until they are thoroughly coated. Leave in a cool place to marinate for 30 minutes.

2 Meanwhile, heat the oil in a wok or skillet, add the cashews and fry until golden brown. Drain on paper towels and keep warm.

3 Add the turkey and marinade to the wok or skillet and stir-fry for 2 minutes. Add the mushrooms and cook for 1 further minute. Pile the mixture on to a warmed serving dish and sprinkle with the cashews. Serve immediately.

Serves 4
Preparation time: 5 minutes, plus marinating
Cooking time: 6–7 minutes

PEPPER AND FENNEL MARINATED GOATS' CHEESE

The herbs and spices added to the oil infuse the goats' cheese as it slowly marinates,
resulting in a delicate and delicious flavor.

1 cup goats' cheese

Pepper and Fennel Marinade:
1 teaspoon fennel seeds
1 teaspoon pink peppercorns
2 garlic cloves, peeled
2 small green chilies, bruised
2 sprigs rosemary, bruised
2 bay leaves, bruised
extra virgin olive oil, to cover

1 Put the fennel seeds and peppercorns in a small, heavy-based frying pan and heat gently until they start to pop and release an aroma. Leave to cool completely.

2 Roll the goats' cheese into small balls and place them in a bowl or jar. Add the cooled fennel seeds and peppercorns, then add the remaining marinade ingredients with sufficient olive oil to cover the cheese.

3 Store in a cool place to marinate for at least 3 days, but for no longer than 1 week. Serve the cheese balls with a little of the oil and chunks of crusty bread or slices of toasted French bread.

Serves 6–8
Preparation time: 15 minutes, plus marinating

MARINATED EGGPLANT

1 pound eggplants
½ cup water
1¼ cups white wine vinegar
whole wheat toast, to serve (optional)

Oregano and Garlic Marinade:
2 tablespoons lemon juice
2 tablespoons extra virgin olive oil
2 garlic cloves, minced
2 teaspoons chopped oregano
1 teaspoon chopped green chili
1 tablespoon capers
salt and freshly ground black pepper

1 Peel and thinly slice the eggplants lengthwise. Put the water and vinegar in a saucepan, cover, and bring to the boil. Add the eggplant slices to the pan, a few slices at a time, and simmer until the color and texture of the eggplants begin to change. Drain well and repeat the process until all the slices are cooked.

2 Mix together all the ingredients for the marinade, add the warm eggplant and leave to marinate for 24 hours.

3 Drain the eggplant and serve it at room temperature with warm, whole wheat toast, if liked.

Serves 4

Preparation time: 10 minutes, plus marinating
Cooking time: 5 minutes (per batch)

MARINATED ARTICHOKES

If small globe artichokes are not available, you can marinate larger cooked artichoke hearts in the same way.

1 lemon, quartered
1 bay leaf
1 teaspoon dried thyme
2 garlic cloves, peeled
24 small globe artichokes, not more than 2 inches wide

Lemon and Parsley Marinade:
1/2 cup olive oil
3 tablespoons lemon juice
2 tablespoons orange juice
1 tablespoon red wine vinegar
1 teaspoon Dijon mustard
1/2 teaspoon dried green peppercorns, crushed
2 tablespoons diced red bell pepper
2 tablespoons chopped fresh parsley
1/2 teaspoon dried oregano
salt

1 Half-fill a large saucepan with cold water. Squeeze the juice from the lemon quarters into the water, then add the lemon quarters with the bay leaf, thyme, and garlic.

2 Trim the stem of each artichoke level with the base. Pull off the outer leaves until all are pale green, then cut off the top third of the artichoke. As each artichoke is prepared, drop it into the pan of water.

3 When all the artichokes have been prepared, bring the water to a boil. Cover the pan, lower the heat, and gently simmer for about 20 minutes, or until the artichokes are just tender. Remove from the heat and leave to cool in the cooking water.

4 Drain the artichokes and cut each one in half lengthwise. Drain them, cut sides down, on paper towels for a few minutes, then arrange them, cut sides up, in a large, shallow serving dish.

5 Beat together the ingredients for the marinade in a bowl. Pour evenly over the artichokes, then cover and marinate at room temperature for at least 2 hours before serving. Serve with chunks of crusty bread to soak up the extra juices.

Serves 6–8
Preparation time: 25 minutes, plus marinating
Cooking time: 20 minutes

MARINATED CUCUMBER, RADISH, AND DILL SALAD

2 cucumbers
6 tablespoons sea salt
1 bunch radishes, trimmed
and thinly sliced
1 egg yolk
1 tablespoon coarse-grain mustard
1 tablespoon clear honey
2 tablespoons lemon juice
3 tablespoons olive oil
3 tablespoons chopped dill weed
freshly ground black pepper

1 Cut both the cucumbers in half lengthwise, scoop out the seeds, and slice very thinly.

2 Layer the cucumber slices in a colander and sprinkle with the salt. Set the colander over a plate or in the sink to catch the juices and leave for 1–1½ hours. Rinse well under cold water, drain and pat the slices dry with paper towels. Place in a salad bowl and add the radishes.

3 Put the egg yolk in a small bowl with the mustard, honey, and lemon juice. Season with pepper and beat well to combine. Continue beating while gradually adding the oil in a thin stream until thoroughly blended. Stir in the chopped dill weed. Add to the cucumber and radishes, toss well and leave to marinate for at least 1 hour before serving.

Serves 4–6
Preparation time: 15 minutes, plus salting and marinating

CILANTRO, LIME, AND HONEY MARINATED TOMATO SALAD

2 pounds tomatoes, sliced or quartered
2 teaspoons grated lime zest
$\frac{1}{2}$ small red onion, thinly sliced
I tablespoon sesame seeds, toasted

Cilantro, Lime and Honey Marinade:
2 tablespoons chopped cilantro
I tablespoon lime juice
I garlic clove, minced
$\frac{1}{2}$ teaspoon clear honey
pinch of cayenne pepper
salt and freshly ground black pepper
4 tablespoons extra virgin olive oil

I First make the marinade. Beat together the cilantro, lime juice, garlic, honey, cayenne, and oil, and season with salt and pepper.
2 Arrange the tomatoes in a large serving bowl and scatter over the lime zest, red onion, and toasted sesame seeds, if using.
3 Beat the marinade ingredients again and pour over the salad. Cover the salad and leave to marinate for 30 minutes for the flavors to develop, before serving.

Serves 4
Preparation time: 5 minutes, plus marinating

MARINATED BELL PEPPER SALAD

A colorful accompaniment to hot or cold meats. Peeling the bell peppers takes away the bitterness and also helps them to absorb all the delicious juices of the marinade.

I garlic clove
6 tablespoons oil
3 tablespoons wine vinegar
¼ teaspoon ground coriander
I teaspoon sugar
salt
freshly ground black pepper

Salad:
I red bell pepper
I green bell pepper
I yellow bell pepper
cilantro or parsley, finely chopped, to garnish

I Peel and crush the garlic to a smooth paste with a little salt. Mix well, adding the oil, vinegar, ground coriander, sugar, and pepper.
2 Halve and deseed the bell peppers. Place under a preheated broiler, skin sides up. Cook until the skins blister, then remove from the heat and peel. Cut the bell peppers into thick strips and arrange, alternating the colors, on a large serving platter.
3 Spoon the marinade over the bell peppers, then cover loosely with plastic wrap. Leave in a cool place for 4 hours. Garnish with the finely chopped cilantro or parsley.

Serves 6
Preparation time: 15 minutes
Cooking time: 5 minutes

LEMON AND THYME MARINATED MUSHROOMS

½ pound large flat open cap mushrooms

Lemon and Thyme Marinade:
1 small lemon
6 tablespoons olive oil
1 tablespoon thyme leaves
or 1 teaspoon dried thyme
1 tablespoon chopped parsley
1 small garlic clove, minced (optional)
salt and freshly ground black pepper

1 Slice the mushrooms crosswise into long thin strips and arrange them in a shallow serving dish.

2 Grate the zest of the lemon into a mixing bowl and add the squeezed juice. Beat in the olive oil, thyme, parsley, garlic, and salt and pepper.

3 Pour the dressing over the mushrooms and leave to marinate for at least 1 hour. This dish can be prepared several hours in advance. Cover and keep chilled.

Serves 4
Preparation time: 10 minutes plus marinating

VARIATION
For a more substantial salad add 2 cups peeled shrimp or flaked tuna.

CHILI AND SOY MARINATED OLIVES

2 cups mixed whole green and black olives
I garlic clove, minced
I teaspoon grated ginger
2 lime leaves, shredded, or grated
zest of I lime
2 red chilies
2 tablespoons dark soy sauce
extra virgin olive oil, to cover

Place all the ingredients in a bowl and stir well. Cover and leave to marinate in the refrigerator for up to 1 week.

Serves 6

Preparation time: 5 minutes, plus marinating

VARIATION

BALSAMIC MARINATED GREEN OLIVES

Use this marinade if you prefer the bitter-sweet taste of balsamic vinegar.

2 cups large whole green olives
2 garlic cloves, minced
grated zest of ½ lemon
I tablespoon balsamic vinegar
½ teaspoon chili flakes
4 tablespoons extra virgin olive oil

Place the olives in a bowl with all the marinade ingredients and stir well. Cover and leave to marinate in the refrigerator for up to 3 days.

Serves 8

Preparation time: 5 minutes, plus marinating

VERMOUTH MARINADE WITH ZUCCHINI KEBOBS

6–8 large zucchini
16 cherry tomatoes

Vermouth Marinade:
¼ cup olive oil
¼ cup dry vermouth
1 tablespoon lemon juice
1 garlic clove, minced
1 teaspoon Worcestershire sauce
few drops of angostura bitters
freshly ground black pepper

1 Trim the ends off the zucchini, then slice lengthways with a vegetable peeler.

2 Combine the marinade ingredients, with black pepper to taste, in a bowl and beat lightly together. Add the strips of zucchini and the cherry tomatoes and stir to coat with the marinade. Cover and marinate in a cool place (not the refrigerator) for at least 1 hour, stirring occasionally.

3 Drain the vegetables, reserving the marinade. Fold and thread the strips of zucchini on to skewers, using the cherry tomatoes to secure the ends.

4 Put the vegetable skewers on the grill over medium hot coals and cook for about 10 minutes, turning and basting with the reserved marinade until just tender but still crisp. Serve warm.

Serves 6–8
Preparation time: 15 minutes, plus marinating
Cooking time: about 10 minutes

INDEX